A HUNGER FOR LEARNING

A Creative Minds Biography

A HUNGER FOR LEARNING

A Story about Booker T. Washington

by Gwenyth Swain

illustrations by Larry Johnson

M Millbrook Press/Minneapolis

Millbrook Press
A division of Lerner Publishing Group
241 First Avenue North
Minneapolis, MN 55401 U.S.A.

Website address: www.lernerbooks.com

Library of Congress Cataloging-in-Publication Data

Swain, Gwenyth, 1961–
    A hunger for learning : a story about Booker T. Washington / by
  Gwenyth Swain ; illustrations by Larry Johnson.
        p.   cm. — (A creative minds biography)
    Includes bibliographical references and index.
    ISBN-13: 978–1–57505–754–5 (lib. bdg. : alk. paper)
    ISBN-10: 1–57505–754–9 (lib. bdg. : alk. paper)
    1. Washington, Booker T., 1856–1915—Juvenile literature. 2. African
Americans—Biography—Juvenile literature. 3. Educators—United
States—Biography—Juvenile literature. I. Johnson, Larry, 1949– ill.
II. Title. III. Series.
E185.97.W4S93 2006
370'.92—dc22   2005010078

Manufactured in the United States of America
1 2 3 4 5 6 – JR – 11 10 09 08 07 06

Table of Contents

1

Slavery Days

What do you remember from when you were young? Probably a whole lot. Booker T. Washington had strong, long-lasting memories of his childhood. He was most likely born in 1856. But since he was born a slave, no one thought to record his birth. He always celebrated his birthday in springtime, around Easter. When he was a child, he belonged to a Virginia farmer named James Burroughs. And for as long as he lived, Booker T. Washington never forgot what it was like to be a slave.

Slaves in the 1850s and 1860s, when Booker was little, couldn't do much of anything without their master's say-so. Booker's stepfather, Washington Ferguson, who belonged to the farmer across the road, could only come to visit when Master Burroughs allowed it, usually just once a year. Booker's brother, John, was three and a half years older than Booker. John could only leave the farm when Master ordered him to drive the wagon to town for mail or supplies or to take Master's daughter, Miss Laura Burroughs, to the little one-room school where she taught. Booker's mother, Jane, could only give her children a pile of rags for a bed on the dirt floor. Even baby Amanda, three years younger than Booker, had to sleep on rags. That's all Master Burroughs thought slaves needed for comfort at night.

Booker could only learn what Master thought he should know. All Master thought a slave boy should know was how to obey. Booker couldn't learn reading or writing. Most masters thought a slave who had book learning was a slave who might run off. It was against the law for Booker to try to learn his ABCs. It was against the law for anyone to try to teach him.

If Booker ever thought about doing anything Master didn't allow, he could see plenty of examples of why it was risky, too risky for a small boy. The proof came when Master raised his whip. As far as Booker could tell, Master whipped grown slaves—

strong men like his uncle Monroe—for things that seemed no worse than learning to read. Even when Booker was all grown, he couldn't forget Uncle Monroe's cries of "Pray, master! Pray, master!" when the cowhide whip cut into his bare back. In all his years as a slave, Booker never got a beating or a whipping. You could call him lucky, if you didn't know how it felt to be a slave.

Master Burroughs wasn't particularly bad or good. He was average in cruelty. He gave Booker's family a cabin to live in. But he didn't fix the gaps between the oak logs or make sure the door held on its hinges well enough to keep out the cold winter air. In summer, with Jane's cooking fire burning in the open fireplace, the cabin was hotter than a furnace. It stayed hot even at night, when Booker sweated and tried to sleep.

Master kept his slaves fed, but it wasn't a healthy diet. Most days, it was a crust of bread, a chunk of meat, or milk drunk by all from a single cup. Booker's mother grew weak and worn-out from poor food and from her work as Master's cook. But she did her best to keep her children healthy, even if it meant taking things Master would never give freely to a slave. One night, Jane woke her children and whispered, "Hush!" In the dark of the cabin, she handed them hot chicken legs and thighs, fresh from the fire. Booker never asked where she got the chicken. He never mentioned the late night treat to Master.

Master gave his slaves clothes to wear, but the cloth was so rough and rude it tore at the skin. Slave boys like Booker got a new shirt to wear every year. The shirt hung down to Booker's knees, so Master felt no need to give the boy pants. Booker's brother, John, knew how scratchy those shirts felt up against tender young skin. He wore each new shirt for a few days until it was broken in for Booker.

Booker knew that some folks—white folks—lived differently. As soon as he was old enough, Booker worked in the "big house." Master's house wasn't the biggest in Hale's Ford, Virginia. But it had wooden floors and big rooms heated by brick fireplaces.

In the big house at mealtimes, Booker pulled a cord that moved a set of fans, keeping flies away from the food. While Booker tugged and tugged on that cord, he watched the Burroughs family eat, sitting on chairs around a table. To a boy who had never taken a meal sitting down (unless squatting on the dirt floor of a slave cabin counts), dinner in the Burroughs's house was a wonder. How could folks manage to eat such a variety of breads, meats, potatoes, corn, and cobbler all at once?

Whispers around the slave cabins said that Booker was the son of a white man, someone with wood floors, chairs to sit on, and plenty of food to eat. But Booker's father never took an interest in his son. If he saw the boy with gray eyes and reddish hair around Hale's Ford, he never asked Booker's master if he could take the boy home and raise him. When Booker was little, the only kinds of fathers he knew were his stepfather, Wash, who visited at Christmastime, and Master Burroughs, who ordered Booker around every day. When Booker was just five years old, Master Burroughs stopped ordering the slaves around. He was too sick.

It was 1861, and more than just the Burroughs farm was changing. When John picked up the mail, he always lingered long enough to hear what the white folks were talking about. John's "grapevine telegraph" brought the latest news and gossip to the slaves before anyone in the big house heard about it. That spring there was plenty of news.

In April the state of Virginia voted to leave the Union, or United States. Virginia joined with other states in the South to form a different country called the Confederacy. The capital of the Confederacy was right in Virginia, at Richmond. In July soldiers from the Confederacy fought Union soldiers in a Virginia town called Manassas. The Confederacy won this first major battle of the Civil War.

Booker understood some of what he heard from the grapevine telegraph and some of what he overheard at the Burroughs's dinner table. The war, he learned, was being fought partly over slaves just like him. Slavery had been against the law in the North for several years. If the Confederacy, based in the South, won the war, then slavery would surely continue and probably spread to more states. If the Union, based in the North, won the war, then slavery would end. Booker and his family might be free.

In 1861 freedom seemed far, far away. There were more important concerns right at home. On July 24, Master Burroughs died. Not long after, two of his sons, Master Billy and Master Frank, joined the Confederate army. Mistress Burroughs, helped by Miss Laura, took charge of running the farm. Running a farm in good times was hard. In wartime the Burroughs women struggled.

Any extra food produced on the farm went to feed the army. Any extra wool made uniforms and blankets for soldiers. Any extra hides from cows or pigs made bags to keep soldiers' gunpowder dry or shoes for soldiers' feet. It didn't go to the Burroughs ladies or to their slaves. At Hale's Ford everyone suffered, but as far as Booker could see, maybe the whites suffered most. They were used to extras like coffee and tea and white sugar. Booker had never known such luxuries, so he didn't miss them.

Booker didn't get out of his usual work just because there was a war on. Since the farm was shorthanded, he did other chores on top of his regular ones. Sometimes, when John was busy, Booker escorted Miss Laura to school. He followed behind her, carrying her books. When she was safely to the school, Booker took the reins of her horse and led it back to the farm, where all work animals were needed.

For Booker, this errand was always bittersweet. Inside the school, he saw boys and girls his own age bent over books or writing on slates. Just by looking, Booker could tell this was something he dearly wanted to do. Book learning looked as good as freedom sounded. But the school where Miss Laura taught was for whites only. Maybe all schools were.

Back at the farm, Booker went right to work. He and the other slaves worked hard every day but Sunday, all year, until Christmas. At Christmastime no one worked for at least a week. Christmas was a time of nearly enough rest and nearly enough food, the only time like it in the year. It was also a time for presents, even for slave boys like Booker.

In 1864, when Booker was eight and a half, he had the best Christmas yet. The war continued, but the grapevine telegraph said the South was losing. Could freedom be far off?

Wash, Booker's stepfather, didn't come to the Burroughs farm for Christmas as usual, but Booker and everyone else knew where he was. Wash had decided not to wait for the North to win the war. He'd run off and found freedom on his own in West Virginia, a state where slavery was illegal. If slavery ever ended in the South, Booker and his family would have a place to go.

Even better than the news Booker got that Christmas were the presents. He put his stocking by the fire, as he always did. When he rose—well before the others, at four o'clock in the morning—he found his mother's nicest ginger cakes, some red store-bought candies, and a pair of wooden-soled shoes. Booker was a boy, but this last present told him he was nearly a man.

Booker had never owned a pair of shoes before. The hard hickory soles rang out like shotgun blasts on the flagstones around the big house. Booker loved the way those shoes sounded. He loved the way they fit. He loved the way they kept his feet warm and dry, all winter long and into that spring.

Booker didn't know it when he first tried on his new shoes that Christmas, but this would be his last Christmas at the Burroughs place in Hale's Ford. And these were the shoes he would wear when, finally, he was free.

2

Freedom

What did it mean to be free? At first, that morning when the slaves gathered at the steps of the big house at the Burroughs farm and heard the news, freedom meant happiness. Shouting and whooping and hollering happiness. General Robert E. Lee, leader of the Army of the Confederacy had surrendered, and the long war was over. Slaves were free!

But sometime after that spring day in 1865, newly freed slaves on the Burroughs farm began to wonder. Where would they live? Where would they find work, and how would they get there? What kind of work could they do? Would they be paid money?

How would the grown-ups feed their children? Freedom, Booker came to realize, was a serious matter.

As bad as slavery had been, it was the only life Booker, his brother and sister, and his mother had ever known. So for a time, they stayed on at Hale's Ford, still living in the slave cabin, still working for Mistress Burroughs. In August, Booker's stepfather, Wash, sent money for the whole family to travel from southwestern Virginia to Malden, West Virginia, nearly two hundred miles away.

When Booker arrived in Malden, a small town in the Kanawha Valley, he knew just what he wanted to do. He wanted to learn to read and write. But even though freedom had come to southern blacks, there were few schools for them. There were schools around Malden, but like the schoolhouse where Miss Laura taught back in Hale's Ford, these schools were for whites only. Booker and other newly freed blacks hoped and prayed that a school for them might open soon. But Malden's blacks didn't have a building, a teacher, or even books to read.

Booker didn't have time to figure out how to get an education. Almost the moment he arrived in Malden, Wash found him a job. Booker was only nine and a bit small for his age, but he was old enough to earn money at the Kanawha saltworks.

It wasn't easy money or easy work. But it was the kind of work people had been doing around Malden for nearly seventy years.

If you took a drink of water from a well or a spring in Malden, you'd pucker your lips. The salt in the ground made the water that salty. Booker didn't do the heaviest work of shoveling the dried, crystallized salt into barrels. Wash did that part. But Booker and his brother, John, helped with the packing and pounding. Only by packing the salt in hard could you fill the barrels well enough to please the packing boss. Even then, you didn't make much money. Booker started work before the sun was up and didn't quit until nearly dinnertime. The little he earned—along with Wash and John's pay—was barely enough to cover rent on a cabin. Jane, Booker's mother, took in washing to cover the family's other costs, and his sister, Amanda, helped her out.

Booker couldn't keep from wanting more, even when he knew his family had almost nothing to spare. One day he asked his mother for a book. Booker wanted to read so much that he didn't care what kind of book it was.

Somehow Jane managed to grant his wish. Saving money from her washing, she bought a ragged blue black spelling book to put in Booker's hands. There were letters in it, all right, but they didn't make sense to Booker. He knew no one in the saltworks or on his street who could tell him what all the *ab*'s and *ba*'s meant. So he settled for studying the book on his own, hoping that the longer he studied, the clearer its meaning might be.

One day a former Union soldier named William Davis arrived in Malden. Davis was a black man, and he could read. Wasn't he just the fellow to teach, if Malden could ever put together a school? Pastor Rice of the black Baptist church in Malden solved the riddle of where to have the school. He gave up his own bedroom, pushing back his mattress to make more space. With a teacher and a room, Malden's school was ready to open, for surely a book or two would follow where students were so determined to learn.

What Booker wouldn't have given to be a student in that first class in Pastor Rice's bedroom. How he pleaded with Wash to let him go to school. How he tugged on his mother's sleeves and begged, when it was clear Wash wouldn't let him.

The answer was always the same. The new school wasn't free, and Booker's family couldn't afford to pay the small fee for classes. What's more, they couldn't spare the money Booker earned. He had to work. They all did. What hurt most was watching students head off to school each day. Booker could see the smiles and the sun on their faces. He vowed to join them.

Booker did become a student, but not during the day. He convinced Mr. Davis to take him on as a student at night. Then, somehow, Booker found money to pay for those nighttime lessons. Many schools for former slaves held night classes. Those classes were flooded with eager students, ranging in age from six to sixty-six and older. Everyone, it seemed, was hungry for learning. Booker loved his lessons, but his first class posed a problem. All the other students had at least two names.

When Booker was born, Master had called him Bowker, the name of another farmer in Hale's Ford. That Mr. Bowker was most likely Jane's first owner. Soon Bowker had become Booker. Jane had given him another name, Taliaferro (TAHL-luh-ver), after another local family. She'd used the name so rarely that Booker had forgotten he'd ever had it. When Mr. Davis asked his name in class, Booker called out the best two names he could come up with on short notice, Booker Washington.

He liked the sound of it—his first name and his stepfather's first name, Washington, put together. Later, when Jane reminded him of his other name,

Taliaferro, Booker made it his middle name, then shortened it to the initial *T*. Put together, Booker T. Washington was a fine name. Booker dreamed of being as important as his name sounded.

For a time, Booker Washington's stepfather let him go to day school. During those few short months, Booker rose early to be at work at four o'clock in the morning. He stayed until nine, when the school bell rang. Then, after lessons ended in the afternoon, he was back packing salt with his brother, John, for a few more hours. But even putting in seven or more hours of work each day, Booker wasn't earning enough. Soon he was back at work all day, going to night school only when he could afford it. How would he ever get the schooling he'd been dreaming of for so long?

3

Working for Mrs. Ruffner

Life might be easier, Booker reasoned, if he could find better-paying work. Sometime in 1867, he thought he'd found it. General Ruffner, the owner of the saltworks, had a big white frame house and an even bigger garden. His wife, Viola, needed a house-boy and gardener. Booker would earn five dollars each month for his family doing work that sounded a whole lot easier than packing salt. Maybe Booker didn't know how many houseboys Mrs. Ruffner had gone through. He surely didn't know until his first day on the job how hard Mrs. Ruffner was to please. And he didn't know—until she showed him the dirt he'd missed on the floor and the weeds he'd left in the garden—just how hard working for her could be.

At first, it was more than Booker could take, and he ran off, looking for better jobs. Once, he worked as a steamboat cabin boy on the Kanawha and Ohio rivers. But after the boat made its run to Cincinnati and back, Booker returned to Mrs. Ruffner's white frame house and asked for his old job back.

Viola Ruffner was strict, and her tone with Booker was nearly always harsh and demanding. But Booker also learned that she was fair. If he did his work well, she gave him no complaints. If he didn't do his work well, he heard all about it.

Booker learned that Mrs. Ruffner liked things kept clean and in good repair. He didn't know how to do that at first, but Mrs. Ruffner was willing to show him. When he tried on his own, he often asked her, "Am I getting on?" Slowly but surely, Booker started getting on as Mrs. Ruffner's houseboy.

It got to the point where, he remembered later, he couldn't stand to walk by pieces of litter—stray papers or trash—and "not want to pick them up at once." Grease stains on clothes had the same effect on him. So did broken fence posts and peeling paint. He couldn't pass them by without itching to clean or fix them. Mrs. Ruffner had taught him to do tasks well.

She also taught him to do tasks promptly in order to keep things from falling apart and going to ruin.

After a time, the Ruffners asked Booker to be Mrs. Ruffner's live-in servant. Mrs. Ruffner was often moody and unhappy. Being with her all day, Booker couldn't help but notice how lonely she was. Viola Ruffner was the general's second wife. She'd come to West Virginia from New Jersey, where she had run her own school, to tutor General Ruffner's youngest children. When the two married, the general's children did not approve.

Viola Ruffner taught Booker things she might have taught her stepchildren, if only they had let her. Along with teaching him to take care of the house and garden, she taught him how to make money. When fruits and vegetables from her large garden began to ripen, Booker would load them into a wagon. Then he would stop at every little house along the road from Malden to Charleston and sell Mrs. Ruffner's garden produce. He kept a close accounting and made sure to give her every penny earned. Honesty, Booker knew, was something Mrs. Ruffner valued more than just about anything else.

Yet, as much as Booker learned from Mrs. Ruffner, he still sometimes found it hard to live and work under her roof. When he was a teenager, he ran off again. Not far from Malden was a coal mine where Booker had worked before. He was soon loading coal onto carts and leading the mules that pulled heaping carts through the mine's tunnels and back into daylight and the world aboveground.

Hauling coal was dirty, hard work. The only good thing that came from it was a conversation Booker overheard between two older miners. They spoke about a school for blacks in Virginia where you might go if you had learned all your local teacher could teach you. Even if you didn't have money to pay for your room and food, you could go there. But you had to work for the school if you wanted to stay in it. From what the miners said, Booker figured you had to work hard.

Booker was no stranger to hard work. But he didn't see how he was ever going to get to the school—called the Hampton Institute—working all day in a mine until he was too tired to think. Before long, Booker was at Mrs. Ruffner's door asking, once again, for his old job back. Perhaps Viola Ruffner was lonely for the boy's company. Perhaps she thought he was finally there to stay. She rehired him as her house and garden servant.

She encouraged Booker to read books and study at night when he had finished his work. In the winter, when Booker didn't have to drive the vegetable wagon, she allowed him to go for a few hours to Malden's school for blacks. There, he met the school's newest teacher, Henry Clay Payne. Mr. Payne taught Booker as much book learning as he could in the short winter months. And perhaps without realizing it, Mr. Payne also taught Booker to keep on dreaming about school.

Booker discovered that Mr. Payne had studied at the Hampton Institute, the same school the miners had described. Once he'd met a graduate of the school, Booker just *had* to get to the Hampton Institute. But it was five hundred miles away. Where would he find the money to travel so far? How could he leave his family and Mrs. Ruffner behind? How could his family spare the money he earned? It seemed like an impossible dream. But if Mr. Payne could do it, maybe Booker could too. By the fall of 1872, when he was sixteen years old, he was ready to try.

4

At Hampton

Just getting to the Hampton Institute was a struggle. With help from his mother, his brother John, and other blacks around Malden, Booker collected enough money to take the train halfway. From that point, he made his way by stagecoach. When his money ran low, he traveled on foot. By the time he reached Richmond, Virginia, only eighty miles from Hampton, Booker had no money left. He could walk the eighty miles if he had to, but he needed some money to survive. To feed his hungry belly, he got a job unloading a boat. To keep the rain off his back at night, he slept under a wooden sidewalk.

Booker was dusty, tired, and broke when he finally arrived at the Hampton Institute on October 5, 1872. Classes had already started for the fall term. No one knew what to do with him at first. But then the head teacher, Miss Mary Mackie, asked him to sweep a classroom. It was a kind of admissions test, and Booker meant to pass it. He swept that room as if Mrs. Ruffner were watching. Even when he was sure the room was clean, he swept it again—and again. Then he found a rag and dusted everything in sight.

Miss Mackie looked over Booker's work. She tried to find some missed speck of dust or dirt. She even took a white handkerchief to the walls and tables. But soon she had to stop and say, "I guess we will try you as a student." To pay his board, Booker would work as a janitor in the school's main building, three stories of red brick. To pay his other expenses, well, he hoped he'd find a way. He had fifty cents left.

One way or another, Booker found a way to attend the Hampton Institute. All the other students were up at five o'clock at the sound of the "rising" bell. Booker was up at four, making sure the fires were lit and all the rooms were clean and ready for the day. He finished work by 5:45 so he could stand with others for inspection. Students who wanted to stay at Hampton learned early that every shirt button had to be sewn on tight. Every collar stain had to be cleaned away. And every shoe had to be polished.

After inspection, Booker spent mornings studying reading, writing, and math. He also learned geography, bookkeeping, and civics. After lunch and roll call, it was back to classes again. Booker marched with the others from class to class and then kept right on marching at military-style drill in the afternoon. At Hampton, there was a time for everything: morning prayers at 6:30, recess at 10:20, evening prayers at 6:45, and study hours until just before the "retiring" bell at 9:30.

Living at Hampton was a bit like living in a military camp. Even some of the buildings were leftover barracks where Union troops had lived when they were stationed in the area. But the main reason for the military flavor, Booker learned, was the school's founder, General Samuel C. Armstrong. During the Civil War, Armstrong was one of the Union's youngest generals. Even though he was white, he'd led black troops. After the war, he'd worked among free blacks, finally establishing a school for them, the Hampton Institute.

Like Viola Ruffner, General Armstrong was strict but fair. Booker remembered later that "there was something about [the general] that was superhuman."

He was so tall and proud and good. Others at Hampton agreed. When the school had no room for new students, Booker and others told the general they'd be happy to live in tents until rooms could be built. General Armstrong's visits to the tents that winter warmed Booker's spirits, even when the cold winds whipped through the flaps and pulled tent posts from the ground. It felt good to be helping the general and helping the school.

As much as Booker gave to Hampton—rising early to clean the rooms, spending cold nights in a tent—the school gave him back even more. General Armstrong found a northerner willing to pay for Booker's classes. Miss Mackie gave him summer work just when he worried that he'd never earn enough to return. Another teacher, Miss Lord, gave him free lessons in public speaking. (Booker told her he hoped to become a lawyer or a preacher, and he needed to know how to talk to a crowd.)

Most importantly, Booker saw how students and teachers at the Hampton Institute thrived when they had work to do and took the time to do it well. Not just schoolwork, but all work. How could Booker forget the look of satisfaction on Miss Mackie's face when she helped him clean all three floors of windows at the main building before the first day of classes? Miss Mackie was a well-educated white woman from the North. But like Booker's former boss, Viola Ruffner, she wasn't too high and mighty to pick up a rag and scrub. However much he learned, Booker hoped he never forgot that lesson from Mrs. Ruffner and the Hampton Institute—that work made you feel good inside. When that work was scrubbing windows, it made the outside world look good, too.

In three short years, Booker finished his courses at the Hampton Institute. On graduation day, a class-mate remembered later, Booker looked like a con-queror who had just "won a great victory." But what would his next fight be? First, Booker returned home to Malden, West Virginia. His mother had died, but the rest of his family was still there, still struggling. Booker soon got a job teaching in the same school he'd worked so hard to attend. He earned enough to send John to the Hampton Institute. And he gave special tutoring to students he thought might follow in his and John's footsteps. He started a night school for students who had to work during the day and Sunday School classes for those who wanted to learn from the Bible after church. But even though he loved his work, Booker longed for something more.

In 1878, when he was twenty-two years old, Booker

left Malden for Washington, D.C. He studied for a while in a seminary, a school that trains ministers. But students there spent all their time reading books. Booker missed the hard work that had been such an important part of life at Hampton. How, he wondered, could ministers hope to help their congregations if they didn't value *all* work? In frustration, Booker gave up his dream of becoming a minister.

He was still searching for direction when General Armstrong asked for his help. Hampton needed a new teacher, someone who could inspire the night school students to stay awake and learn their lessons. Just as Booker had done when he was growing up in Malden, these students worked long hours during the day. By nighttime they were exhausted. But General Armstrong was sure Booker T. Washington was the man who could fire them up to learn.

Mr. Washington affectionately called his night school students the "Plucky Class," to show how much he appreciated their "pluck," or their willingness to fight for the chance to learn. He was not the kind of teacher who earned a nickname from his students, but that didn't mean they didn't like him. Once they had been studying with Mr. Washington for a good while, each student received a certificate of Plucky Class membership "in good and regular standing."

While Washington taught, he also learned. General Armstrong allowed him to attend classes or take lessons to fill in any gaps in his education. When the general received a letter from Alabama asking for a qualified man to lead a new school to train black teachers, the choice was clear. Booker T. Washington was as qualified a leader and teacher as the Hampton Institute could offer.

"The only man I can suggest," the general wrote, "is one Mr. Booker Washington, a graduate of this institution. . . . The best man we ever had here. I am satisfied he would not disappoint you."

General Armstrong could be very persuasive, as Booker T. Washington well knew. But Washington also knew that the men in Alabama had not asked for a black teacher. They had asked for a white man to lead the new school for blacks. General Armstrong told them in his letter that Booker Washington was black—"a very competent capable mulatto" as he put it. But he had also made it clear that Washington was the man for the job. "I know of no white man," he wrote, "who could do better." Would the men in Alabama believe General Armstrong?

A week passed before an answer arrived. The telegram was short and to the point. "Booker T. Washington will suit us. Send him at once."

5

Building Tuskegee

Tuskegee. Even the name sounded foreign to Washington. It was an old Creek Indian name meaning "warrior." The Creek Indians no longer lived in Tuskegee, Alabama, nor did many other people. It was a small town far off the beaten path. In June of 1881, when Booker T. Washington got off the train at the nearest station, he still had five more miles to go before he saw the home of his new school.

He looked hard but didn't see much at first. Where was the school? No land for it had yet been purchased. Where were the teachers? None had been hired. Where were the books and desks and chairs?

Nowhere to be seen. Still, Washington wrote back to the Hampton Institute that very day saying, "The place has a healthy and pleasant location—high and hilly. Think I shall like it. Will open school 1st Monday in July."

In July 1881, the first Monday was Independence Day. Booker T. Washington planned to make this Fourth of July extra special for blacks around Tuskegee. He hastily wrote to the Hampton Institute asking for any schoolbooks and other supplies that might be spared. "You know what I need," he wrote, "and *any thing* that you can send me I will be thankful for."

Many blacks in Tuskegee were also ready to help Washington. Lewis Adams, a former slave and Tuskegee businessman, drove Washington to a one-hundred-acre farm for sale south of town. The only buildings on the land were a pair of outhouses, a henhouse, an old slave cabin, another small cabin, and a stable. But Adams and Washington agreed it would be the perfect site for the new school. Until money could be raised to buy the land, members of the all-black African Methodist Episcopal Church in Tuskegee offered Washington a small shanty in town to use for a classroom. And both of the two local black churches invited Booker T. Washington to speak to their congregations about the new school.

In spite of many obstacles, Washington managed to open Tuskegee Normal School for Colored Teachers on July 4, 1881. Normal schools trained students who wanted to become teachers, mainly in elementary schools. Washington's thirty students not only wanted to become teachers, many already *were* teachers. But however much they had already studied, they knew they needed more schooling to stay ahead of their students. They were eager to learn whatever Washington could teach them.

"Well," one student remembered later, "that first class was wonderful. We just knew nothing worth knowing. . . . Booker just got hold of us, and the first week he was busy classifying us. Some knew nothing; there were some who were well enough along to be juniors in college. Then he just overhauled us."

The "overhaul" started with things Washington had learned at the Hampton Institute, such as the importance of keeping clean. Male students rushed out to buy the white paper shirt collars and dark neckties Washington required. Everyone had to have a toothbrush and use it. (Washington told the story of three female students with one toothbrush between them. "Yes, sir," they told him. "That is our brush. We bought it together yesterday." Washington soon set them straight.)

Washington also overhauled his students' views about work. With a loan from the Hampton Institute, Booker purchased the farm on which he planned to build a permanent school. He asked the male students to help him clear the land. After classes each day in spelling, history, and grammar, Washington grabbed an ax and led the way. "Every man had to take his ax and cut and cut until they was near dead and there was a lot of cleared land and plenty of wood laying about," a student remembered. The female students cleaned up the henhouse, cabins, and stable, turning them into classrooms. Whether they were cleaning henhouses or chopping wood, students learned from Washington that their work was important—just as important as any work they did with books in the classroom.

Like Washington, many students were former slaves. A few had the idea that being free and educated meant not having to do hard physical work. Tuskegee lost some students when Washington handed out axes and brooms, but even more students arrived who were willing to work hard.

Soon Washington needed more staff. That fall he convinced two teachers, both Hampton graduates, to join him in Tuskegee. Then he hired his brother, John. Hampton graduate Olivia Davidson arrived next to take the job of lady principal. She went to work at once raising money for books, desks, and buildings. The Alabama state legislature had set aside two thousand dollars for the school, but that money was for teacher's salaries. Students paid for their room and board and tuition if they could, but most "worked off" their expenses in jobs around school. Davidson searched for ways to pay for expenses that student fees and state funding didn't cover.

Black and white residents of Tuskegee got used to hearing Miss Davidson's polite knock on the door. Could they bake a pie for the next fund-raising supper? Might they make a donation to help pay off the loan for the school's land? No donation was too small. Washington and Davidson never forgot the old former slave who donated six eggs she'd saved to help educate the "boys an' gals" of Tuskegee.

Washington started his school's jobs program with farming, because "we wanted something to eat." Before long, students also worked caring for the school's goats and sheep and hogs and cows. Students even earned their way through school by building the school. They dug foundations, learned brick making and bricklaying, and painted and finished buildings inside and out. (Years later at class reunions, former students often stopped to touch the bricks they had made and put in place.)

Washington was proud of his students' work, and he wanted to share the story of the school they were building with others. After the first year of classes ended, Washington left Tuskegee for the summer. He traveled through Massachusetts and other northern states talking about the school and asking for donations. Washington believed so firmly in Tuskegee and its mission that he was a convincing speaker. Slowly but surely, donations arrived at the school.

In the fall of 1882, a new face arrived at Tuskegee as well. During his summer travels, Washington had convinced Fanny Norton Smith, a new Hampton graduate he'd first met in Malden, to become his wife. Even with a new wife (and soon a daughter named Portia), Washington didn't slow down the pace of his work building the new school.

In 1883 Washington started night classes, creating Tuskegee's own version of the Plucky Class. Washington hired more and more teachers, all black and many graduates of the Hampton Institute. By the end of 1884, the school, soon known as the Tuskegee Normal and Industrial Institute, enrolled a record 169 students. By the mid-1890s, numerous buildings dotted the campus. Porter Hall, the first major building on campus, was joined by Phelps Hall, Science Hall, a blacksmith's shop, a foundry, and a large brick chapel. Out of nothing, it seemed, Booker T. Washington, his students, and his staff had created a school for black students, taught by black teachers and built from the ground up by black labor.

But there were problems along the way. In 1884 Fanny Washington died suddenly from injuries from a fall. Booker's second wife, Lady Principal Olivia Davidson, died in 1889 after giving birth to their second son. But even as a single father of three children—Portia, Booker Jr., and Ernest—Washington forged on, throwing himself into his work.

Each year there was the question of whether the legislature would set aside money again so the school might remain open. Legislators were white, and Tuskegee was a school for blacks. Not all white Alabamans thought educating blacks was a good idea. Not all wanted Tuskegee to remain open.

Washington got a taste of how some white Alabamans viewed Tuskegee when some of his teachers went for a train ride. Two had just married, and all were in good spirits. They were dressed in their best and sat in the best car in the train. At a stop, several white men surrounded the car yelling, "Put 'em off!" The white men didn't like seeing blacks riding in the first-class car, and the teachers didn't dare stay. They moved back to the dirty, sooty car for black passengers.

Washington complained in a letter to a local newspaper that the train company should provide a first-class car for blacks, just as it did for whites. "Let them give us a separate one as good in every particular and just as exclusive, and *there will be no complaint.*" To get along with his white neighbors, Washington never insisted that blacks and whites should be together—not on train cars and not in schools. Instead, he argued that if each race had separate facilities that were just as good as the other's, then everyone would be happy. The problem was, train companies were slow about adding first-class cars, or even clean third-class cars, for blacks. And the Alabama state legislature never set aside as much money for Tuskegee as it did for schools for whites.

Others might have pointed out such unfairness, but that wasn't Washington's way. Instead, he tried to be a good neighbor to white Alabamans—the kind of neighbor who never said anything upsetting. In time, he hoped whites might come to see that he was worthy of their respect. He had won Mrs. Ruffner's respect and General Armstrong's respect. He wasn't going to stop there, not if Tuskegee were to survive and prosper.

6

A Voice for the South

In 1895 Booker T. Washington was asked to speak at the Cotton States and International Exposition in Atlanta, Georgia. Washington had appeared on the same stage with whites at important gatherings in the North before. But, he later wrote, "This was the first time in the entire history of the Negro that a member of [his] race had been asked to speak from the same platform with white Southern men and women on any important National occasion."

Many white southerners were familiar with Washington and his message. They were satisfied that he wouldn't take advantage of the opportunity of being on a large stage to complain about the situation of blacks in the South. That situation was rapidly worsening. In the late 1800s, a series of laws made it more and more difficult for southern blacks to claim their rights as citizens. These so-called Jim Crow laws forced blacks to pass tests before they could vote and kept blacks from sitting where they wished on trains and in other public places. They even controlled where blacks could be buried—separate from whites.

Washington planned to make no complaints about Jim Crow laws. He did not wish to anger southern whites or to offend any northern whites who made donations to the Tuskegee Institute. At the same time, however, he swore that he would "say nothing that [he] did not feel from the bottom of [his] heart to be right and true." He was very aware that many blacks would be in the crowd, even if they were allowed to sit only in the farthest balconies. His new wife, Maggie Murray Washington, and his three children would also be sitting there, eager to hear him speak.

Only thirty years had passed, Washington reminded his audience, since the end of slavery. Washington had never forgotten what it felt like to be a slave. But his struggles to make something of his life and to found Tuskegee had taught him important lessons. Southern blacks, he insisted, shouldn't think they could start "at the top." Rather than setting their sights on a seat in the legislature, they should start a dairy farm. Instead of writing poetry, they should learn to plow fields. Instead of arguing for the right to vote in an election, southern blacks should concentrate on buying their own homes, educating their children in useful trades, and building a stronger South from the ground up. "It is at the bottom of life we must begin," Washington said again and again.

Washington knew that southern whites were often reluctant to hire blacks. They suspected these former slaves or sons and daughters of slaves of being "uppity," or as Washington put it, wanting to start "at the top." In Atlanta, Booker T. Washington tried to put those suspicions to rest. Blacks and whites, he urged, could work closely in business, on farms, and in factories. But they needn't be forced together in schools, at the voting place, in restaurants, or in other social settings. Holding his hand high, his fingers spread apart, Washington put it this way: "In all things that are purely social we can be as separate as the fingers . . ." Closing his fist he went on, ". . . yet one as the hand in all things essential to mutual progress." As Booker stood with his fist still raised in the air, the crowd began cheering. From the farthest balconies, those cheers rolled through the whole auditorium.

Booker T. Washington had set out a dream for a peaceful South, a new South in which blacks and whites might work together as "friends." But it wasn't a South where blacks fought for their right to vote, to attend schools alongside white students, or to sit somewhere other than the farthest balconies. Washington valued those rights, but he valued the right to work more. He figured that once southern blacks rose to prominence as shopkeepers, farmers, or bricklayers, southern whites would grant them the respect and rights they deserved.

From the start, southern whites welcomed Washington's "Atlanta Compromise." Blacks were more mixed in their response. It was a fine thing to have a black man light up the stage and electrify a crowd the way Washington did in Atlanta. But some people questioned whether the compromise was a good one.

"The opportunity to earn a dollar in a factory just now," Washington said in Atlanta, "is worth infinitely more than the opportunity to spend a dollar in an opera house." Most blacks wouldn't argue with Washington on that point. But was the opportunity to earn a dollar worth more than the opportunity to vote? Many American blacks would have firmly told Washington no.

Whether the compromise Washington suggested was good or not, his speech in Atlanta did great things for Tuskegee. Newspapers around the country covered Washington's role at the opening of the exposition. Soon whites, north and south, overwhelmed him with requests for more speeches. His five minutes on the stage in Atlanta made Booker T. Washington "National," as he put it later. It made the Tuskegee Institute "National," too. Donations poured in. Blacks and whites who had never heard of the school were suddenly reading all about it.

Anyone who heard Washington speak or who read about him in a newspaper wanted to learn more. In 1901 Washington wrote a book about his life called *Up from Slavery*. Washington didn't write the book alone. He was far too busy. But with help from a longtime Tuskegee employee, Max Thrasher, he pulled together the story of his life. *Up from Slavery* was an instant success.

One person who read the book and enjoyed it was President Theodore Roosevelt. In the fall of 1901, Roosevelt invited Washington to dine with him and his family at the White House. It was a dinner both were to regret. Southern whites, as Washington knew, did not care to see blacks meeting socially with whites—particularly not with the president.

Washington's southern white supporters lashed out at him for what they saw as a "blunder." President Roosevelt also heard complaints for having invited a black man to his personal quarters. Many white voters, south and north, felt uncomfortable with the idea that the president had shared his family dinner with a former slave. Roosevelt downplayed the importance of Washington's visit, although he continued to talk with Washington when he had questions about blacks and the South.

Washington's Atlanta Compromise speech, his autobiography, and his dinner at the White House all served to make him the most famous black man of his time. Many people saw him as the spokesmen for all American blacks. But many blacks objected, saying that no single person could reflect the variety of black ideas and experiences.

Some criticized Washington for the "darky" stories he told when he spoke before white audiences. Many whites of the day found these stories funny. But many blacks thought the stories portrayed them as childish fools. Others criticized Washington's philosophy and teachings.

In 1903 the black leader W. E. B. Du Bois wrote a book called *The Souls of Black Folk*. In an essay in the book, Du Bois rejected Washington's emphasis on building farms, starting businesses, and buying property. Instead, Du Bois urged blacks to seek the vote and other rights of citizens first, before working for economic equality. Du Bois also insisted that while learning a trade might suit some blacks, it did not suit the talents and goals of all blacks. He pointed out that Washington's emphasis on blacks working with their hands pleased southern and northern whites, many of whom believed that blacks were too ignorant to do other work.

Such criticisms stung Washington. But he didn't let them distract him from his work for Tuskegee Institute. What started in a shack next to the local African Methodist Episcopal church had become a thriving collection of teachers, students, and large and sturdy buildings. In the early days, rain leaked through the shack's roof so much that a student usually stood by Washington, holding an umbrella over his head so he could teach. As Tuskegee grew and prospered, students still held an umbrella over their principal on rainy days, but only when he was walking outside. The students thought it an honor to carry anything for Washington—an umbrella, a pile of books, a coat.

In 1915, at the age of fifty-nine, Booker T. Washington died. His school, however, lives on.

From thirty students in 1881, the school has grown to more than three thousand. Students from around the country and around the world attend what has become Tuskegee University. In spite of rapid growth and a new name, the school's leaders still believe that "students should select Tuskegee University based upon educational considerations and not financial factors," just as Washington would have wanted.

Bibliography

Books and Articles

Harlan, Louis R. *Booker T. Washington: The Making of a Black Leader.* New York: Oxford University Press, 1972.

Harlan, Louis R. *Booker T. Washington: The Wizard of Tuskegee, 1901–1915.* New York: Oxford University Press, 1983.

Harlan, Louis R., ed. *The Booker T. Washington Papers.* 14 vols. Urbana: University of Illinois Press, 1972–1989.

St. Paul Dispatch 28 (January 14, 1896): 7.

"Starting Tuskegee." *Literary Digest* 51, no. 23 (Dec. 4, 1915): 1307–1310.

Thornbrough, Emma Lou, ed. *Booker T. Washington.* Englewood Cliffs, NJ: Prentice-Hall, 1969.

Washington, Booker T. *The Story of My Life and Work.* Naperville, IL: J. L. Nichols & Company, 1901.

Washington, Booker T. *Up from Slavery.* New York: Penguin Books, 1986.

Websites

Booker T. Washington National Monument Home Page
http://www.nps.gov/bowa/
Learn about Booker T. Washington's birthplace.

History Cooperative
http://www.historycooperative.org/btw/index.html
Read the entire fourteen-volume *Booker T. Washington Papers* and view photographs.

Tuskegee University
http://www.tuskegee.edu/
Learn about the school started by Booker T. Washington.

All quotations in this biography were taken from the above sources.

Index